HOPELESSLY
hopeful
DURING SEPARATION

Endorsements

I was only two months old the day my father separated from my mother. Too young to recognize her tears. Too young to understand the deepening hurt as her separation turned into divorce. I wish my mom would have had Mollie's book. I wish you didn't need it. But if you're in that emotional "no man's land" that is too often separation, this is unlike any book I've ever read. I've never seen a book specifically for this painful, confusing season that is so personal. So real. So faith encouraging, yet so hard to read in places because of its honesty. But important to read. Not all at once. But day after tough day. Twenty-eight days of hope, reality, and encouragement. Full of hard-earned wisdom. Like Mollie says, "You're not alone." May the Lord reveal for you a path to health, healing, and life over the next four weeks and beyond.

John Trent, Ph.D.
President, StrongFamilies.com
Author of *LifeMapping* and co-author of *The Blessing*

God has a purpose for us. Our trials and troubles result in suffering which the apostle Paul in Romans 5:3-4 says causes us to "grow in perseverance." In Mollie's devotional, *Hopelessly Hopeful During Separation*, she reveals stories about how faith can be strengthened through the trial of a relationship gone south. Leveraging her God-given gifts, she shows how you can conquer that failure. Mollie is now using her personal testimony as an inspiration to others. Her writing inspired me as I went through a divorce twenty-five years ago, so I understand her pain. This devotional will continue to be a place for me to go to for encouragement.

Diane Paddison
Founder and Executive Director of 4word, www.4wordwomen.org
Author of *Work, Love, Pray and Be Refreshed...a year of devotions for women in the workplace* and Former Global Executive Team of two Fortune 500 and one Fortune 1000 companies

Separation is a state of limbo in which you are vacillating between hopeful and hopeless. All kinds of feelings, questions, and confusion arise. These devotionals from true-life stories reveal that you are not alone and that can provide you a community of hope—hope that is found in the Lord.

Paula Silva
President, Cofounder
FOCUS Ministries, Inc. | www.focusministries1.org

As a divorced woman, I wish that I had something like *Hopelessly Hopeful During Separation*. To know my thoughts, fears, and pain are real and experienced by others as well. To feel like I could walk with someone on this journey and to know that I am not alone. That's what this book does for its readers. The stories are inspiring, and Mollie brings the Word of God to life and makes it practical to our current life experiences. Thank you, Mollie, for walking with your readers no matter the outcome.

Christine Soule
Founder and CEO of Providence Heights
Author of *Broken and Beautiful*

Hopelessly Hopeful During Separation is like a breath of fresh air during a trial that anyone may be going through. It provides a "turning point" solution to life's challenges. Anyone who is going through a dark valley and difficult circumstance can find sweet intimacy with Jesus and a bright light at the end of the tunnel. I believe as you read and reflect on the devotions, you will find yourself encouraged, empowered, and filled with hope despite the giants you are facing. This book contains gentle and truthful guidance as well as hope in any situation.

Isik Abla
Founder and President of Isik Abla Ministries
TV & Social Media Evangelist
Author and Pastor of Dream Church

This is the book I wish I'd had during the hardest season of my life. Dr. Mollie Bond provides a powerful combination of hope and practical steps that will both inspire and encourage you. Mollie has walked through the painful and personal journey of healing, and she has come out whole, healed, and restored. Her vulnerability, faith, and gentle guidance will help you do the same. I can't think of a better resource to help encourage you during the hard days ahead. Hope and healing are possible, and I pray you experience both, and God's redemptive love, in each page as you spend the next twenty-eight days on a powerful and transformational journey with Mollie. I can't think of a better guide to help you along the way.

Kari Trent Stageberg
CEO of StrongFamilies.com
Co-Author of *The Blessing*

Living in day-to-day separation from a spouse can be one of the most painful journeys in life. As one tear-filled day blurs into another, the future may appear bleak and any entertainment of a brighter tomorrow seems cruelly unrealistic. However, the book you have in your hands is full of wisdom and inspiration and has been walked out by Dr. Bond personally. She is the kind of nonjudgmental, experienced sojourner you need, offering Scripture and responsive prayer as lights to help guide the reader forward as only a friend who has "been there" can do.

Jennifer Hayden Epperson, EdD
Author of *The Pioneer's Way*
www.jenniferhaydenepperson.com

HOPELESSLY
hopeful
DURING SEPARATION

28 Daily Devotionals of Hope for
Those Experiencing Marital Separation

Mollie Bond

Ambassador International
Greenville, South Carolina & Belfast, Northern Ireland
www.ambassador-international.com

Hopelessly Hopeful During Separation

28 Daily Devotionals of Hope for Those Experiencing Marital Separation
©2021 by Mollie Bond
All rights reserved

ISBN: 978-1-64960-125-4
eISBN: 978-1-64960-175-9

Cover Design by Hannah Linder Designs
Interior Design by Dentelle Design
Edited by Megan Gerig

Scriptures taken from the Holy Bible, New International Version®, NIV®. Copyright © 1973, 1978, 1984, 2011 by Biblica, Inc.™ Used by permission of Zondervan. All rights reserved worldwide. www.zondervan.com The "NIV" and "New International Version" are trademarks registered in the United States Patent and Trademark Office by Biblica, Inc.™

No part of this publication may be reproduced, distributed, or transmitted in any form or by any means, including photocopying, recording, or other electronic or mechanical methods, without the prior written permission of the publisher, except in the case of brief quotations embodied in critical reviews and certain other noncommercial uses permitted by copyright law. For permission requests, contact the publisher using the information below.

AMBASSADOR INTERNATIONAL
Emerald House
411 University Ridge, Suite B14
Greenville, SC 29601, USA
www.ambassador-international.com

AMBASSADOR BOOKS
The Mount
2 Woodstock Link
Belfast, BT6 8DD, Northern Ireland, UK
www.ambassadormedia.co.uk

The colophon is a trademark of Ambassador, a Christian publishing company.

Additional Endorsements

This is a book that I wish I had years ago when I was in a season of separation. Mollie's authenticity invites us to meet with and know a God Who sees, hears, and is very present in dark and confusing times. Dear one, you are not alone.

Sarah Kardelen
Advocate, Therapist, and Founder of Tapestry Therapy

The world says discouragement should separate us from God—cause us to question His love for us or even deny His existence. Christ says the opposite: grief, pain, and sorrow are paths back to the heart of our triune God. *Hopelessly Hopeful During Separation* does a masterful job of reminding us of that truth. Mollie Bond's memorable prose strikes enduring notes of empathy and encouragement—a much-needed balm for all readers.

Kristina Cowan
Author of *When Postpartum Packs a Punch: Fighting Back and Finding Joy*

Contents

PREFACE 13

1
ARE YOU OKAY? 17

2
COOKING A POT OF BITTERNESS 21

3
ACKNOWLEDGING WEAKNESSES 25

4
GOD'S RELATIONSHIPS 29

5
THE TURNING TRIANGLE 33

6
WALKING BY BOWING DOWN 37

7
IS THERE A FUTURE? 41

8
PLANNING 45

9
WHO CAN I TRUST? 49

10
MEMORIES 53

11
BEING QUIET BEFORE GOD 57

12
DON'T LET YOUR SOUL ROT 61

13
BOUNDARIES 65

14
DARK CLOUDS 69

15
VITAMINS 73

16
WHAT TO LOSE 77

17
WONDERING HEART 81

18
WORDLESS STORIES 85

19
TAKING CARE OF FAMILIES 89

20
REACH FOR GOD 93

21
FIND YOURSELF IN GOD 97

22
I CAN'T WANT THAT 101

23
FINDING ANSWERS 105

24
EXPECT TROUBLES 109

25
OPINIONS 113

26
FINDING YOUR INNER CIRCLE 117

27
GOD'S RESTORATION 121

28
BENEDICTION 125

ACKNOWLEDGMENTS 127
BIBLIOGRAPHY 129

Preface

The newlywed shine had worn off my white gold ring months ago. I looked down at the white plastic grocery bag in my lap. Everything I possessed was in that bag—the extra underwear and toothbrush I purchased the night before, plus my identification and the twenty dollars I had just pulled out of the ATM. I wrapped the coat gifted by a friend even closer, although the June heat had kicked on outside. A nurse sat beside me, both of us stand-by passengers on a June flight to the heartland of America.

My nurse friend talked about her job, and I told her that maybe someday I could help another human too. But not in the state I was in. "Why?" she asked me.

I quit my job three months before and found a part-time job. My husband was unemployed for the third month in a row. Finances were tight. The twenty dollars was the last of the funds for me, and I had left him twenty dollars in the account. My parents bought me a plane ticket; it was time to get out. Adultery and controlling behaviors exhibited by both of us had put me here. I slept the night before at a friend's house, leaving the car so that he couldn't track me, and my friend drove me to the airport, saying that our common employer would understand if I called later that day as to why I abruptly left my job.

Another friend, Paula, (whom I was previously "not allowed" to talk to) had treated me for a quick sandwich earlier that day. I was putting us at risk, I knew, and thought about it as we drove to an obscure location to talk. I tried not to gobble down food, somewhat a luxury. But at the same time, I was so sick to my stomach that while we sat at the park and watched the softball leagues play, I cried and tried to wrap my mind around what was happening. I was separating, long-term.

The flight attendant called my name. I walked on the plane, holding in tears, as I passed my nurse friend who just smiled at me. I was on my way to a new start. Still, I wonder today, what if someone had told me in the prior months that there was hope for even me? That my life didn't have to be like this? That God was close and that He cared? I knew I was bitter, but I just couldn't see the light at the end of a tunnel. There was no exit until I saw that nurse's smile. A bit of hope.

And that's what I offer to you. A bit of hope, a smile when it seems like your life will never change.

Once I arrived at my parent's house, I slept a lot, I cried a lot, and I had permanent PMS. Since I was unemployed, I read books constantly. I had a tough time finding a book that would hold my hand and answer the questions I couldn't quite figure out on my own. This book developed out of that month to encourage those who are newly separated.

Please note that I am not a trained counselor. I also do not have all the answers as your questions might be different than mine. Circumstances could also make your separation look different. For example, my ex-husband and I had no children. So, I can't speak about some issues other newly separated people face. Your situation is unique, but don't give up hope. If you look to Jesus as your source of hope, you will come out of this season stronger, no matter if your future holds reconciliation or divorce. As you grow closer to God, through prayer and listening to Him, you will find your answers. You are not alone.

The following stories are from those who have willingly shared their story with me and have given me permission to share with you. We've all agreed it's important to share these tidbits so that you may know that many have experienced the pain of being separated. All names have been changed, but all experiences are true.

But let this small book hold your hand and be your friend as you travel through the next month. Some days will be more challenging than others, but remember that turning to God's Bible is the best source of encouragement. Stay in the Word as long as you need, but make sure you do it daily. If the Bible doesn't make sense, start here with these few words. This book has twenty-eight devotions, which means there is support for you seven days a week for four weeks.

You are not alone. Let's seek hope together.

1
Are You Okay?

How long, Lord? Will you forget me forever? How long will you hide your face from me? How long must I wrestle with my thoughts and day after day have sorrow in my heart? How long will my enemy triumph over me? But I trust in your unfailing love; my heart rejoices in your salvation. I will sing the Lord's praise, for he has been good to me.

Psalm 13:1-2, 5-6

Sleepless nights, dark circles under my eyes, the questions: "Are you okay? Where is he?" I couldn't answer them. Not for a whole month. We were still married, but I did not know where my husband was for a month.

During the one month alone, I wept on the phone. I read Psalm 13 over and over. "Will you forget me forever?" I echoed. That night, my friend stayed up with me and cried until we saw the sun rise. Then I went to work. The questions started again. One month. I hadn't seen or heard from my husband for one month.

Even now I cannot say for certain where he stayed, whom he was with, or if I did the right thing. We did eventually come back together—for about a year before I left permanently. During the time he was away, I *do* know that I needed someone to walk me through the dry wasteland, encouraging me to be right with God before even attempting to be right with my husband.

In the end, our situation ended with divorce. Today, I have no gut-wrenching feelings when I check the "divorced" box on medical forms. I had a friend, named Jesus, who walked me through my sorrow and began my healing, even before the separation began.

This month-long devotion is designed to be a friend to walk you through your sorrow. My situation is not yours, but maybe learning the lessons I wish I had known will encourage your heart. This devotion can weep with you and hold your hand when the questions come—from others and from yourself.

Then we will rejoice together, because even the Psalmist of Psalm 13, David, came out singing after sorrow. David had worship after wrestling. David trusted after he had others triumph over him. One day at a time, even if it is for a month.

God,

Today, I am alone. Will You forget me? Your Word says no, so I will trust it. Your Word also says to rejoice in my salvation. So today, I choose to focus on You because You have been good to me.

2
Cooking a Pot of Bitterness

They refused to listen and failed to remember the miracles you performed among them. They became stiff-necked and in their rebellion appointed a leader in order to return to their slavery. But you are a forgiving God, gracious and compassionate, slow to anger and abounding in love. Therefore, you did not desert them.

Nehemiah 9:17

Erika was a war wife. While her husband was at war, she wrote letters on occasion, in between the phone calls. She told me seeing the word "free" in place of a postage stamp with the APO address was almost like a letter that was sealed with a kiss.

Sometimes the letters were angry, full of true emotion. Sometimes the letters were sad, announcing things cryptically since secret information couldn't always be divulged. But those letters were read over and over again, smelled, tucked under pillows, and hugged. The letters wrapped two hearts together.

Letters are the physical evidence of happy memories. Erika and her husband were apart, but the letters kept them together and were the basis of happy memories.

Later, as Erika experienced a separation, she mentioned the letters to me. It was her way of remembering the good times, not to relish in unrealistic memories, but to recognize how God weaves the good with the bad (Ecclesiastes 7:14). I admired her courage; she could have let her thoughts become filled with hate and bitterness (anger that has stewed for too long). Instead, she wanted to forgive and to let go. Her memories, or the negative feelings attached with those memories, did not return her to slavery. She was free through God.

Erika's attitude of gratitude for God's forgiveness inspires me to remember His grace and compassion. If He were none of these things, if He was more like us, then He would have deserted us long ago. But God never left Erika once during those long months of separation. Perhaps it felt that way, but in the end, He was right beside her, both while her husband was away at war and during their separation later in marriage.

God won't leave you either. Allow God to forgive, remembering the good He has done for you. Anger is a horrible slave driver. Don't throw out the letters, or the good memories, to cook up a good pot of bitterness.

Father God,

Sometimes I fail to remember the good You have done in my life. I appoint another leader to ruin my life, then I cling to the bitterness left behind. Please forgive my attitude and me. I know You are gracious and compassionate, and I'm glad You promise not to leave me. Be with me as I face today.

3
Acknowledging Weaknesses

Moses said to the Lord, "Pardon your servant, Lord. I have never been eloquent, neither in the past nor since you have spoken to your servant. I am slow of speech and tongue." The Lord said to him, "Who gave human beings their mouths? Who makes them deaf or mute? Who gives them sight or makes them blind? Is it not I, the Lord? Now go; I will help you speak and will teach you what to say."

Exodus 4:10–12

Cynthia showed me the wrinkled and charred journal. During a fight, her spouse tossed her journals into the barbeque pit, splashed them with lighter fluid, then set them on fire. A stroke of consciousness caused her spouse to douse the fire with water. However, only one journal was recovered, and that journal held prayers, verses, or ideas dedicated to her marriage. Cynthia told me about the journal because a spark of an idea came to her years after her marriage ended. Could she use the journal as a way to remember and forgive? She started writing prayers in a new journal. At first, the prayers were angry. But then the softer tone dripped from the ink. What caused the change?

When Moses tried to use his faults to get out of his destiny, God did something that we glance over many times: He acknowledged Moses's weakness. What made this tremendous is that God chose not to fix Moses's mouth, which He certainly could have done; instead, He gave Moses help in the form of a friend.

Cynthia used writing as her mouth when she couldn't speak of the cruelties in her home. Writing ignited a change of heart.

Cynthia's story caused me to reflect on my own. I remember when my prayers were harsh and angry. I wanted God to fix my situation. I wanted Him to change it to what I desired. I wanted someone else to do it for me. I remember realizing I needed to pray for myself too: "Lord, change me. Don't change him because I want him to be a better leader, to speak more proficiently, to love on me more. Change me to be more like You and help me to know what to say." Cynthia's notebook, and God's Scripture, taught me that He's not in the business of fixing what annoys us; He's in the business of fixing attitudes.

Cynthia's story encouraged me to pray kindly for husbands when I talk to other women experiencing separation. "Lord, keep him safe" was sometimes the only thing I could say. Then I'd pray, "Teach us what to say, not to change another person into what we want." I learned the weight of God's words to Moses.

If you sign divorce papers or take that drive back home, I encourage you to pray lightly for your spouse and heavily for yourself. Not for a fixer-upper, but for a change of attitude. Start now and don't stop.

Lord Jesus,

I want to be a better servant for You, not for me. I want to be a better person for You, not for me. And I want to be a life-giver for You, not for me. I pray my words will be from the heart, and more so that my heart is pure before You. Cleanse me from the nasty emotions I've kept. I'd rather burn away those selfish thoughts. I'm ready to give it over to restore life.

4
God's Relationships

Whoever would foster love covers over an offense,
but whoever repeats the matter separates close friends.

Proverbs 17:9

"How many times will I ask before the truth sinks in?" Corey cried one day after church. She and I sang in the choir together, and I had asked where her husband, Aaron, was sitting. We had just performed our Easter special, and there was one service left. During practices, she told me of her separation, but Aaron said he would see her sing on Easter. We were catching up between performances.

Corey went on, "Every Saturday evening, I ask Aaron if he wants to come to church with me. Every Saturday he says yes, and then by Sunday morning, I'm driving to church alone." The tears flowed.

I remembered those Sundays. I remembered seeing Aaron from time to time and later hearing from Corey, "Oh, he had a rough week and is staying at home."

During that Easter morning, Corey clung to her phone. She told me that she had been calling Aaron, hoping that he'd make the effort on a special morning to see her sing. The hope he'd call to say he was on the way kept the phone in her hands while we talked. Still, it was clear to both of us—he was not coming to see her sing.

Corey shared with me that before she and Aaron were dating, there was an Easter brunch at a mutual friend's home. Corey left early, and Aaron left shortly after she did. Apparently, he mentioned to a friend that there was no reason to be there unless Corey was there. A sweet sentiment, but as she reflected on that occasion years later, what had changed? The pattern of Corey going to church and pushing Aaron to attend had not changed.

Pushing a spouse to attend church for the sake of appearance is not a good idea. So many want to believe their spouse is a believer to protect their own reputation as a godly person. I knew what Corey was going through. Other motivations may cause the same behavior, but for me, it was that I wanted to be accountable for both of us to God. I clung to the thought that my ex-husband was a drifting but true believer while we were married. This subconsciously protected me against the questions others bombarded me with like, "So, why isn't he here this week?" Early in our marriage at another church, I actually had a pastor's wife tell me to physically hide behind her if someone asked me uncomfortable questions. It was a nice thought, but I couldn't follow through with it. I knew I had to face those questions myself.

The looming question that changed my attitude is why I felt the need to protect my reputation and pretend that I could interfere with the relationship God had with my former husband. By continuing the flaw, I separated two close friends: my God and my husband.

I misinterpreted Proverbs 17:9. In earlier days, Proverbs 17 seemed like two different lessons in the same verse. Covering an offense seemed like hiding sin; however, repeating the lie seemed like a sin in itself. In actuality, this verse promotes forgiveness. Especially when a wrong occurs between two people. It does not dictate that I cover for other people's mistakes. I have to forgive to cover an offense.

I couldn't force my husband to come to church, and neither could Corey force Aaron. Not even on an Easter Sunday when she was singing. Not even if she was at brunch afterward.

It is when we bow down that God can reach a husband's heart. I am responsible for my actions. And in this case, bowing down to God is all I was accountable for.

God forgives, no doubt! We are so fortunate that He cares about us personally. But we must remember that God cares for our spouses too. He will go directly to them. Covering for them is not what the Bible directs us to do; rather, we are to be willing to forgive the offenses made to us personally. Do spouses not go to church to hurt their mate personally? No. Why did I take it personally as if I was God? Proverbs 17 frees me to take responsibility for myself as an individual, not as a couple. Clear up the guilt. Don't separate close friends.

God,

I am getting out of the way so You can do your work. If there is anything my other half has done that I am taking responsibility for, I confess that to You in order to feel Your healing and cleansing. I will promote love in my life and see You promote love in other's lives. I ask that You help me not get in the way, not separate relationships You have with others.

5

The Turning Triangle

Whoever conceals their sins does not prosper,

but the one who confesses and renounces them finds mercy.

Proverbs 28:13

I asked the question one more time, "How much do I tell him?" I asked my counselor, who said, "That's something I can't answer." I asked God, Who said, "Search my Word." For three months, I asked people if I should tell my husband of all the horrible things I had done in our marriage. The backbiting, manipulative, deceitful behaviors that I knew had hurt our relationship.

Then a family member, who usually doesn't strike me as the preachy type, told me about Proverbs 28:13 on the phone. And the feelings struck, just like a lightning bolt. Even though this family member didn't know about my situation, or my struggle of hiding hurtful behaviors from my husband, this verse stuck with me. I tried to ignore it but ended up memorizing the verse because it kept cropping up.

Conviction of the Holy Spirit is like a triangle in your heart. The first turn of the triangle pokes places that cause hurt. But the more times the triangle turns, the pain from the corners lessens. After some time, the corners wear down and the opening around the triangle gets so big that it spins freely, and the pain of conviction wears off.

I asked the question, "How much do I tell him? Should my husband know everything?" For me, I'd received my answer the way God said, through His Word. Proverbs openly lays truths out. If you don't want to prosper, conceal the truth. Want some relief? Then find your mercy in confession. Don't ignore the turning triangle in your heart. Confess it to the Lord. Don't hide it from God.

Some people may insist that you share *all* your sins with your spouse. However, there are some situations where some things need to remain between you and the Lord, especially if the sin does not affect your spouse directly. I have a friend who insists on sharing everything, but that can be detrimental. I have no experience in some of those things she is struggling with, and it only leads me to think about her sin. Instead, through God's leading, I should only confess to the person I've hurt through my sin. In this case, it was my husband. He had the right to respond and to forgive; therefore, only he heard the confession.

If you're looking for the lightning bolt of understanding for your own situation, it won't be the same as it was for me. I know divorced and married people who have not shared their part in the separation, and that was the correct obedience-filled act for them. Still, when you know what God has asked you to do, don't hesitate or back off. Go full force into obedience. Don't ask the question that is holding you back one more time.

Father,

I refuse to simplify my sins and wear them off like a triangle. I will listen to what You are calling me to do in obedience. I want to confess to You because I am so desperate for mercy.

6
Walking by Bowing Down

So then, each of us will give an account of ourselves to God.

Romans 14:12

I heard from a woman who attends my Bible study of a story about her confession. It was the first time her husband had seen the sunrise in years. He walked with his wife down the path, a new kind of date, especially at 7 a.m.! Although a bit chilly to walk so early in March, it must have been refreshing. The winding path, the smell of dew on fresh spring flowers, and the warmth of his hand should have set the woman's heart to an overflow of love. Yet her guilt and shame veiled the love in front of her.

The couple made the last bend toward the car, and she decided to tell him of her affair. "Let's sit here for a moment," she suggested.

He responded, "Let's get to the car to warm up first."

That suggestion almost caused this woman to change her mind, to wait until "the perfect moment" to share what she felt led to discuss. But when they got to the car, she had again made up her mind. Today was the day. As her husband pulled out of the parking lot, she told him of the affair.

Let's be real; it's not fun to confess. She said that his broken heart did not respond well. There was no immediate relief for her, no instantaneous moment of forgiveness from her husband, and definitely not the overflow of love she was hoping to hear from him.

He had his own confession. He had brought a Bible that was now sitting between them on the console. He brought it so that they could read it together after their morning walk. He had sensed something was off.

It sparked in her the memory of when she first sensed the conviction that he should know what she'd done, not in detail, but that she had hurt him. I heard she felt this wave of heat like it was 100°F outside, even in March in Ohio. She said the heat was the burning of conviction in her heart and mind.

She remembered the leader of our Bible study had just started talking about the early years of her own marriage. Submission was the topic for the day, and her story revolved around her not confessing to protect her husband from emotional trauma. As her story dwindled, she said, "I found that submission is not doing what he says. Submission isn't protecting him, standing out in front, and trying to live his life for him. Submission is bowing down to God, mostly so he gets a better aim at my husband." She continued with words that haunted this woman for several more months. "I can't be responsible to mind-read what God wants for my spouse. I am accountable to God for my actions alone. It's God's Word against mine, and God's Word is the one I trust my life with."

This thought correlates with Romans 14. There's no condition. "If you tell then God won't like you" or "If you don't tell then God won't forgive you." God says we are responsible for our own actions. God won't ask what this fellow Bible study attendee did to protect her husband's emotions or keep him from hurting. God will ask if she did what He, as God, asked her to do.

So, was God calling my fellow Bible study attendee to tell? Was she standing out in front, trying to protect her husband, and meanwhile ignoring the signs that she needed to bow down? She would tell you that yes, God asked for her repentance in that car after their walk. It's different for every person and each situation. However, for her, she felt it was costing her honesty in her relationship with her husband and her relationship with God.

This story comes with a happy ending. Days later, her husband responded in forgiveness.

Her story in combination with the Bible study taught me that I am responsible for bowing down. No more, no less. Being obedient to God creates the possibility for God to get a hold of my spouse without my "help." I alone will stand in front of God, and He will ask, "Did you get in my way?" I will give a good account of my time on earth to God.

Whatever your actions are for today, remember to Whom you are accountable and bow down in submission, whatever the call to submission might be for you.

God,

My pride gets in the way of me following what You've asked. Will You provide clear direction as I sort through what I should be doing and what I should be avoiding? I praise You for Your care and desire to see me grow.

7
Is There a Future?

All the days ordained for me were written in your book
before one of them came to be.

Psalm 139:16b

I have heard it before, and I know you have too. You are precious, created in His sight, before the foundations of the world. Sometimes when we are in pain, it sounds like *blah, blah, blah*. I don't make light of the subject. Yet after a wrecked marriage, in my heart of hearts, I wasn't sure who or Whose I was. I couldn't even tell you my favorite color. It came down to this thought, "Is there a future for me? After marriage? At all? Is this the best and I threw it away?"

Studying Psalm 139 changed that line of questioning for me, not reading it from start to finish but paraphrasing each line. In my Bible, I now have a few words about what each line says about God. Not me, but God. A few examples are from Psalm 139:15a which says, "My frame was not hidden from you when I was made in the secret place." Next to it, I wrote, "God knows when I'm awkward." At 5'10" that happens quite a bit. I pondered that for a while, how God is okay with who I am. It helped me see the application. Then I wrote on the other side of the phrase in my Bible, "God had a 'Mollie design/blueprint.'" Now, looking back through these pages, I see I have learned about His love *for me* in my Bible.

This exercise led me to a discovery that my future does matter to God because my past matters to God.

Read Psalm 139. On one side, mark what you learn about God from each phrase or each verse. Then read it again, this time focusing on what it says about the love He lavishes on you, individual you. Let it sink in. No more *blah, blah, blah*.

Father,

I know You care for me, but I want to know in my heart that You care for me. Help me accomplish this exercise so I can see You clearly when I need You the most.

8
Planning

This is what the Lord says to his anointed, to Cyrus, whose right hand I take hold of to subdue nations before him and to strip kings of their armor, to open doors before him so that gates will not be shut.

Isaiah 45:1

I can hear it now in your head. *Yes! Finally, something that will make me feel better. We're going to talk about stripping armor, opening doors, battle!* No, my friend, today is not the day for revenge. It's a day of planning!

I remember the prayers. *Oh Lord, strike him dead.* Or, more frequently (thank God!) *Oh Lord, keep him safe. That's all I can pray.* I was so exhausted during the separation. I remember lying in bed, keeping my eyes closed. Five more minutes of closed eyes were five more minutes of survival. In survival mode, I motivated myself into the shower. And then I took five minutes to motivate myself to the kitchen for breakfast. I took vitamins and felt an increase in energy. Then I continued to motivate myself to get to the next big action in my day. I couldn't live any further than that. And I certainly couldn't live to think about what might happen in the future, let alone tomorrow.

After living this way for a year, I attended a Bible study, not really sure why I was going. I probably went because it was another way to pass the time, another way to survive another day. Isaiah 45:1 dropped into my lap randomly, and I had to do some digging to find where it was in my Bible. This verse to me is all about the future, destiny, and the Master's plan.

King Cyrus was anointed. He had lots of land, he had territories that used to belong to powerful countries: Assyria and Babylonia. He even oversaw the rebuilding of the temple. Cyrus would allow God's people to go back to their homeland if they chose to go, with no leash or pouting or guarantee of anything in return. Cyrus was on God's side.

Two zingers make King Cyrus a memorable character. The first zinger is he wasn't a believer. He did not care about God, or the things of God, but God still had plans for him.

The second zinger is this verse in Isaiah was written 150 years before King Cyrus was born. Now that is destiny! God knows the future.

God knows your future too. Maybe you won't restore a nation, and maybe no one knew of you 150 years ago. (By the way, that would be around 1871 when President Ulysses Grant signed the Civil Rights Act of 1871 and P.T. Barnum opened his circus in New York.) Still, His plans for you were set long, long ago. God cares about you, deeply. He will see you through this if you stick close by His side.

If feelings of confusion enter your mind about the future, go one day at a time. Go one hour at a time. Leave the 150-year timeline to God. He's got you covered.

God,

Cover me as I try to take a hold of my future. Help me to see that if You had something planned for an unbeliever 150 years before his birth, then You have a plan for me, too. Give me hope.

9
Who Can I Trust?

Do not put your trust in princes, in human beings, who cannot save. When their spirit departs, they return to the ground; on that very day their plans come to nothing. Blessed are those whose help is the God of Jacob, whose hope is in the Lord their God. He is the Maker of heaven and earth, the sea, and everything in them—he remains faithful forever.

Psalm 146:3–6

Sam (Samantha) and I split soufflés when we get together. We hadn't connected in so long, and I was surprised to hear she had gone home to her parents' house that summer—for the whole summer. Previously, Sam would go for a week-long visit each summer with an evident heartache that neither she nor I verbalized and come back refreshed with a renewed vigor to heal her marriage. She'd tell me about her new pursuits and ways to "make herself more lovable and acceptable."

Only this time, Sam stayed all summer. And we weren't talking about her love for her husband because he had become her ex-husband. We were discussing what was that pivot point that broke the annual cycle.

Sam's story of that pivotal moment went like this: Over fajitas and chicken wraps at that restaurant—before soufflés—she again announced to her parents, who knew of her broken-beyond-repair marriage, that she was going to be staying for a week or so. It was the tradition they'd all silently come to expect.

She felt caught in between her husband and her parents. Her husband wasn't there to tell his side of the story. Her parents wanted her safe. The tug and pull were invisible and visible. Sam said in that moment she felt overwhelmed with making a huge decision. In fact, she was so overwhelmed, she had let her dad order her meal because the choices before her exhausted her.

Like *déjà vu*, she had her script prepared in her head and laid it out just as before, just as she had planned: "Mom, Dad, I'm going to stay with you, just for a week, but I need to go back to my husband after that. I need to support my husband. God put us together, and I shouldn't be the one to break that up." This time, Sam said she noticed the worry lining her parents' eyes and the scared look they gave each other. Sam saw the silent question passed between them: "*Would* she return?"

Sam's mother paused a moment, took a breath, and rocked Sam's world with a question: "Sam, do you trust him?" And Sam replied without hesitation and without thinking, "No." The word that came from her, as truthful as it was, scared her immensely. She didn't trust her husband?

The Bible has a lot to say about trust. Trust is hard to build back up. That's why God's Word pushes believers to continuously trust in God. Humans fail. They "cannot save" as the Bible says (see Psalm 146:3). Great plans will fail.

Just like Sam's plans of returning to old habits. Somehow in this perfect plan that she designed on her own, her husband would gain instant and rebuilt trust, and everything would turn out okay. But humans cannot save marriages alone.

God created everything we see—our food, our parents, and our marriages. He's got me, and Sam, and He's got you. For me, to trust is to put my plans on hold to see what God's got cooking for me. What's on the menu tonight isn't dependent on me, because I trust the One behind the heat of the grill.

I extend the question to you that Sam's mother asked her, "Do you trust your spouse?" Do you trust your spouse or your plans or your God?

God,

You made my spouse, dreams, desires, and me. As I am feeling my way out, trying to think through some plans that will exalt You, please gently remind me to trust You alone, because You are faithful to me forever.

10
Memories

Though you have made me see troubles, many and bitter, you will restore my life again; from the depths of the earth you will again bring me up.

Psalm 71:20

Crying did not solve matters. It sure did make me feel better though. By being away from my spouse, I knew I was missing big moments in both of our lives that are usually shared—birthdays, holidays, promotions—and even the minor celebrations like a friend's backyard barbecue party. Not all these days held terrible memories. Some were painful, but most days were good. It caused me to go back and forth in confusion on what to do next. So, instead, I cried.

I remember the last meal we shared with friends. Standing on the patio, enjoying the last bit of the summer sun. I can remember the smell of that get-together: the food, the cut grass, his cologne. Why forsake that happy memory for this one I was creating—alone in bitterness and overwhelmed in troubles?

Did I do the right thing? Shouldn't I be at these events, even as his separated wife? What words were my actions speaking?

In that moment, I could only remember three words: feel, deal, and heal. I had to follow the advice of a book read long ago.[1] I felt the sadness, anger,

---

[1] O'Brien, Welby, *Formerly a Wife: A Survival Guide for Women Facing the Pain and Disruption of Divorce* (Camp Sherman, OR: Trusted Books, 1996).

frustration, and confusion. Fortunately, I kept a list of verses that had kept me buoyed in my weepy moments. I pulled out that list and found Psalm 71:20. Although a dreadful day was yet one more ticked off in a row of separation, this day would remind me that God will again make my life good. As they say, when you hit bottom, the only place to go is up. The Bible tells me so.

If today is that bottom day for you, be encouraged that God does not give up, even with past mistakes. Those memories will be just that—memories—in a long succession of newer, happier memories and traditions.

God,

This stretch of bitterness seems endless. But I trust Your Word, and therefore, I trust that You will restore my life in a way I couldn't predict. I love You for watching out for me. Help me to heal, even on the worst of days.

11
Being Quiet Before God

My heart is not proud, Lord, my eyes are not haughty; I do not concern myself with great matters or things too wonderful for me. But I have calmed and quieted myself, I am like a weaned child with its mother; like a weaned child I am content. Israel, put your hope in the Lord both now and forevermore.

Psalm 131

The necklace had big, wooden beads, supplemented by big metal beads. He sat with the necklace two rows ahead of me on the airplane. When I was in high school, I bought a similar necklace. In those innocent days, I bought it with the hopes that if I saw another like it, it would be on the man I married. Although that seems awfully funny now because everyone owned one at the time. Still, I was certain I was going to marry this stranger on a plane. It didn't matter that I was sixteen. Or on an airplane going to Miami. I thought for sure he was "the one." In fact, this is what my journal reads:

"PS I saw the hottest guy on our flight. Slightly older . . . good, simple glasses. Classy shirt and a beaded necklace. It's a nice-looking punk thing."

I have this journal entry because it is in the journal I kept while going on a mission trip. A place I should have been seeking God.

Yet, here I was, headed to "serve God" and still concerning myself with things beyond my control. Quieting my soul takes a lot more than a mission trip. It takes putting my hope in God, remembering that He has great plans for me. Today's verse talks about quieting our souls by trusting God with things beyond us. The destiny He has is too great and too wonderful for me to comprehend. So, throughout the years, I have learned to still and quiet my soul, even when it pants like a sixteen-year-old girl over a "husband" I never married.

I wrote "in light of my husband" next to the chapter heading (Psalm 131) in my Bible, shortly after returning home. I shouldn't be looking for the next man who fits my description of the perfect mate. I should be concerning myself with staying quiet before the Lord and making sure I am hearing Him right. I should trust my God for those things that are way beyond me, like being separated from my husband. Do I understand what God is doing at this time when I am separated? No, but the Psalm directs me to "put your hope in the Lord." So that is what I'll do the next time I see that necklace.

God,

Sometimes I think I know what is best. But You are in control, so I choose to trust You. There are things in progress I do not even recognize, so, I will instead quiet my soul. I hope that You use this time for Your glory.

12
Don't Let Your Soul Rot

Forget the former things; do not dwell on the past.
See, I am doing a new thing! Now it springs up; do you not perceive it?
I am making a way in the wilderness and streams in the wasteland.

Isaiah 43:18–19

I made a point of talking with Carol each week. If not during the time a group of us got together to fold bulletins, then after the weekly Bible study. I grabbed my coffee and went for a hug. This week, Carol threw me for a loop and asked, "What are you memorizing?" Fortunately, the speaker the week before had a verse for us to start memorizing, so I had something to respond with, even if the short passage was imperfect.

In turn, she showed me a post-it on which she had written the first letter of each word of the passage she was memorizing. Squeezing her eyes tight, several verses came from her mouth as her right eye popped open when a word didn't quite find its way out. She was eighty-two years old.

Memorization is so important. Don't take my word for it, check for it in the Word. I hardly doubt there is a verse that says, "Memorization of Scripture will rot your soul, especially if you think it is hard." My inward smile occurs when I hear a person say, "I am too old." I also don't find that in the Bible.

During my separation, I memorized Isaiah 43:18-19. I needed to know there was a destiny for me and that my life wasn't ending at the moment my intimacy ended with my spouse.

Whether you choose Isaiah or another book, use your new free time to get tight with God, Who will be the only One who can see you through. Find a passage in the Psalms that says exactly what you are feeling or thinking. Allow encouragement to squeeze into your heart, even if your eyes are closed.

God,

I can barely focus on what to eat for breakfast, let alone a whole verse. Please give me motivation and a specific verse that helps me to see You for Who You are. Help me to see the new thing You are doing in my life. I feel so dry without You. Show me a new stream in this wasteland.

13
Boundaries

For even when we were with you, we gave you this rule:
"The one who is unwilling to work shall not eat."

2 Thessalonians 3:10

Sandy told me about the time she "stole her car." Her husband left with their only vehicle to stay with his new girlfriend in a town three hours away. The agreement was that as long as he paid the car loan, he could keep the car. Sandy had other means of transportation to get to and from work and removing that debt from her paycheck was a good choice for her.

Then, the pink slip came in the mail. The bank had not received a payment for two months and was notifying her that they would repossess the car if the payment wasn't received by the end of the month. Sandy, once an enabler, made a different choice than what she may have made in the past. The car was in Sandy's name, so she was responsible. Sandy chose to "steal" her own car.

She and a girlfriend pulled into the apartment lot in the middle of the night and found the car. Her friend drove her own car, and Sandy snuck into the other car with her spare key. The next day, she drove it to the dealership where she already had a new car chosen.

As Sandy tells it, she was pulling out of the car dealer lot when the police called. A simple five-minute call established the car was "in her possession," and since the car was registered under her name, the filing that the car was stolen quickly became a closed case.

Sandy's story showed me the power of boundaries. When the notice came in, Sandy called her husband, and he promised to make the payments. Sandy said it would have been so simple to say yes to that request. Time-consuming but less emotional. It was her counselor that showed her today's verse and encouraged her not to take the road that seemed easy.

Sandy's husband had shown patterns of bad choices when it came to money. I remember seeing her husband, who was unemployed, at a gathering with a milkshake in his hand. At the same gathering, Sandy took me aside and asked for ten dollars to pay the electricity bill due the next day. This verse was being lived out in front of me. The hard choice for Sandy was to not make excuses to protect her emotions or his desires but instead obey the Bible, knowing that it says a person has to work in order to eat.

This line of thinking, that no one should enable bad behaviors, is hard to implement if that isn't the pattern. But the Bible is full of verses that show how Jesus healed those who wanted to be healed. They had to walk to the pool to wash their eyes, or they had to give their all to become a disciple. They paid a price because they wanted Jesus.

Although the Bible is also full of examples of men and women who submit, submission is not forgetting who you are and slaving for someone else's handcrafted cookie dough milkshake.

Work for what you need. Not for what others want for you. Build up those boundaries that God protects so that you are protected.

God,

Sometimes it's easier to take the easy route when others ask something of me. I pray my actions instead reflect Your glory, and that I can take a stand when I need to quit enabling poor behaviors.

14
Dark Clouds

For day and night your hand was heavy on me; my strength was sapped as in the heat of summer. Then I acknowledged my sin to you and did not cover up my iniquity. I said, "I will confess my transgressions to the Lord." And you forgave the guilt of my sin. Therefore let all the faithful pray to you while you may be found . . .

Psalm 32:4–6a

I met myself. Sitting outside at a conference, I met a gal who had just separated from her husband, was flirting with another man, and wasn't afraid to admit her anger. I was her just a few years ago. In that moment, it seemed like the sun was blocked by angry clouds.

The words that came from her echoed my past thoughts. "I know what I should be doing, that I should be in the Bible, but I just can't," she confessed. "He hurt me with his affair!"

I had a similar reaction in the last days of being together with my husband. I *wanted* to hurt, to feel justified. Imagine wanting to have the upper hand when I myself had committed wrongs. What a cloud of anger!

I had to get right with God. There was no other way around it. I felt physically tired all the time; I slept for up to twenty hours a day. For each daily task, I thought, "Oh, there's always tomorrow. The sun will come out tomorrow, and I'll deal with it then."

But the author of these simple lines in Psalm denotes an urgent tone at the end of his description of life in sin. The line that says, "While you may be found" (v. 6a) is paraphrased to me as: "Hey, there might be a time when you can't get a hold of God so easily. Get right with Him now before your sin blocks out the Son."

As soon as I came to God, told Him the root of my selfishness, and got over pride, the weight of my anger lifted. The last heartfelt words mimicked a disappearance of a storm cloud I felt obligated to carry around as a self-declared martyr.

Do not think about what your partner has done and the ways you are hurt or angry. It's time to look at you. God will not ask you why your spouse sinned; He'll ask you why you sinned. Get healthy and repent. There may not be time tomorrow. Seek out His forgiveness.

Father,

Give me clear guidance. Give me the humility to let go of my anger and indignation. By not forgiving, I am just as guilty of sin before You. I want to be close to You while I can. Thank You for making a way for me to come to You while You may be found.

15
Vitamins

The angel of the Lord came back a second time and touched him and said, "Get up and eat, for the journey is too much for you." So he got up and ate and drank. Strengthened by that food, he traveled forty days and forty nights until he reached Horeb, the mountain of God. There he went into a cave and spent the night.

1 Kings 19:7–9

It's not easy to "fake it 'til you make it." When I was on the phone with a friend, she challenged me with how I was relaxing during my separation. I had heard the question before, and said, "Oh, well, I'm reading my Bible, and I am doing some things I enjoy." It might have been a lie. I wanted to relax but taking deep breaths seemed so temporary. I'm not into temporary. I was doing these "relaxing" things, but I did not enjoy them, and they were a chore to do. I was tired. And alone.

Then she said, "Well, that's great, but here's what I want you to do. Stop. Take a day, have a vitamin, drink a big glass of water, get some rest. It's good to do what you are doing, but you are not taking care of yourself physically." The best advice I ever got from anyone was to take vitamins.

It reminds me of the story of Elijah, a prophet who needed some vitamins after one particularly difficult season. The Bible says in 1 Kings that, basically, Elijah became a weatherman and announced rain. However, the country was in a drought, so it wasn't well received. King Ahab, who did not believe in God, heard Elijah's words and traveled back to Jezreel to be with his wicked wife Jezebel. Knowing this, Elijah wanted to catch up with Ahab before he met with his wife. Perhaps he wanted to catch Ahab one more time to allow him to turn from sinful behaviors. Or maybe he wanted to make sure that God got the most glory. Either way, Elijah ran. He ran the six miles to Jezreel. He ran and beat Ahab, who was riding a chariot, the clouds building behind him.

After running, Elijah told Jezebel the story. However, she did not appreciate the miracle of rain. So, Elijah ran again. The Bible says, "Elijah was afraid and ran for his life" (1 Kings 19:3a). Sixty miles later, the depression of impending death and physical exhaustion caused him to collapse under a tree, praying to God to take his life. Elijah needed a friend like mine to tell him to take care of himself with some vitamins.

When I couldn't "fake it 'til I made it," I wanted to disappear. I was tired of running. My friend gave excellent advice, and it so happens Elijah experienced similar counsel. Eat. Rest. Get some exercise. I'm not sure I'm ready to travel forty days and forty nights, but a quick walk around the block always does me some good. Then, take a vitamin. Those actions will be life-giving because I won't have to "fake it 'til I make it;" I'll "believe it 'til I become it" and be ready to face the day.

Lord,

I am ready for some rest. Help me to use each moment in the best way possible, even if that means just focusing on eating and resting. I can't wait to see what You are doing outside my doors. Please, show me one small miracle on a walk today.

16
What To Lose

Heal me, Lord, and I will be healed; save me and I will be saved, for you are the one I praise.

Jeremiah 17:14

The hardest concept for me to grasp during the separation was that there was a destiny for me. I couldn't see past tomorrow, let alone the next few minutes. I thought I was stuck forever in a cycle of being hurt.

My friend Kathy was in the same thought cycle. She read David's story and found the consequences of having an affair: David's kingdom was taken away. She looked at me with despair and asked, "David lost his firstborn son. Will I lose my children? David lost his safety. Will I feel safe again?"

It had been years since her affair and subsequent divorce. She couldn't see herself enjoying life again. Someone had to tell her what else David lost.

First, David lost his pride. He humbled himself and told God that he sinned: not against Uriah or his wife, Bathsheba, but against God. He lost himself and gained forgiveness. He accepted the consequences and moved on.

Then David lost his disobedience. Even after his son died, he did not mourn as the servants thought he should have. Instead, he got back on his feet and realized God is the Giver of life and death. That was enough for him to know, and he didn't rebel against God's decision.

Finally, David lost his negativity. Although David had a tough life, he did not lose his beautiful writings in the Psalms. He still praised God. This changed my life and I pray it changed Kathy's, too.

I pass along the same encouragement to you as I mentioned to her. Regardless of the reasons and motivations for your separation, now is not the time to wallow in despair. It is a time to lose pride, disobedience, and negativity. While I was grieving the loss of my job, of my unity with my spouse, I started picking one thing to praise God for each night. It was hard at first. Sometimes I was glad I had a bed. Other times I was glad I saw the sun shining. I was glad for finding independence or for having God with me throughout the tough days. Falling asleep, saying, "God, I'm grateful for the time to focus on You" seemed to chase away angry or anxious dreams.

This spurred me on to two other daily habits. I keep a list of things I can praise God for. It comes in the form of written prayers, one a day. Sometimes they are long, and sometimes they are short. But it keeps me aligned.

It also helped me to memorize the verse above during the separation. Not only to remind me to do my "one a day" but also to trust Him to heal me. There is a destiny for me. The dark days will pass. I can be grateful God won't leave me, and I'll see the sun shining again.

Now it's your turn.

Lord,
   I am thankful for

_____

_____

_____

_____.

17
Wondering Heart

His purpose was to create in himself one new humanity out of the two, thus making peace, and in one body to reconcile both of them to God through the cross, by which he put to death their hostility.

Ephesians 2:15b-16

The wondering was killing my heart. What was he doing? Where was he going? Would I say something wrong? Should I call? Should I wait? Should I go? The questions created the angst of suspicion. I wondered if I did the right thing or the wrong thing. I wondered if I should stay or go. Can reconciliation happen? Was it the best option for me, or should I wait it out?

You cannot reconcile with your spouse alone, only with Christ. It's the truth! This exercise will show how reconciliation works.

Reconciliation is to make amends. If you have a pen close by, draw a cross in the margins. Or picture one in your mind. Write your name on the right side of the paper on the horizontal shorter line and your spouse's name on the left side of the horizontal shorter line. Imagine yourself on that line where you wrote your name. You teeter on one side of the horizontal line, and your spouse on the other, both far away from each other. What is in between you two? A vertical line. If you run to the other side, you'd collide with the vertical line. If you remove it, then once you made it precariously to the other end of the horizontal line, you'd both fall off.

Christ is the vertical line. Reconciliation can be two people coming together as one under God through the cross. Meaning, as you take a step toward the vertical line, drawing yourself nearer to the cross's heart, your spouse must also take a step in that direction. You cannot do it for your spouse. Christ must make peace in you and peace in your spouse, and you will meet in the center under the cross.

A delicate, dangerous, and yet beautiful picture of the cross should cause you to focus on your vertical relationship. Destroy the thought that you both must walk only fifty percent. Both of you must walk one hundred percent toward the center of the cross.

Reconciliation removes the wondering out of my life. Suspicions laid to rest allow me to rest in the knowledge that all I have to do is my part toward getting to the middle of the cross. I have a focus that is my responsibility and allowing God to work through me took care of the rest of the wondering.

Lord Jesus,

I am coming to You today, one hundred percent. You are so gracious to allow me to even be with You! I am fully committing myself to come closer and to lay aside the wonderings. I leave my wondering heart with You.

18
Wordless Stories

Contend, Lord, with those who contend with me; fight against those who fight against me ... Yet when they were ill, I put on sackcloth and humbled myself with fasting ... My tongue will proclaim your righteousness, your praises all day long.

Psalm 35:1, 13a, 28

I had not said one word. In the three months I worked at my new full-time job, I had not told anyone I was married or separated. At the time, I hadn't even contacted a lawyer yet, although I'm sure plenty of people urged me to do so. I didn't feel like I could trust anyone. I didn't know them well enough. Then one girl asked me why on our way to clock out, "Mollie, you are so much fun, but you seem really down today. What is going on?" Since someone noticed me, I took a risk. I longed to tell her that I was separated. I got out one word of the fifty I was thinking, and she said, "Oh, don't worry. There's plenty of men out there, and I'm sure you'll find one." The rambling continued all the way to our vehicles.

Although I was heartbroken, I couldn't share my story, and when I tried, I was cut off. I'm thankful for my friend's gift of gab. If she hadn't interrupted me, I might have shared details no one but my lawyer needed to know. I wanted to fight. I wanted to spill out my hurt, and I wanted to hurt him in the process.

The Bible shares that God contends for those against me. He gets to do the fighting if I'll let Him. So, what do I do in the meantime? The Psalm, which read in its entirety is beautiful, says I treat them as if they were ill. I care for them, I nurture them, and I make sure I do not hurt them anymore.

Most importantly, the Psalm ends by praising God, and I should mimic this attitude. Besides, speaking praises will interrupt my poor word choice and desperate humanistic need to spout others' wrongs.

Could I do that with my separated spouse? Could I care for him when I was so angry? Could I handle the situation in praise when I open my mouth? I may not be able to by myself, but God helped me along the way. The choice saved me heartache and didn't spread the disease of dissatisfaction. Praising God is a much healthier way of living. Even one word of praise covers the fifty words of anger I could have used instead.

God,

I am grateful. I am praising You that You are working in me. I'm glad You are listening to my heart when I have no words. I am going to choose one thing to be thankful for today and praise You for it all day long.

19
Taking Care of Families

You intended to harm me, but God intended it for good to accomplish what is now being done, the saving of many lives. So then, don't be afraid, I will provide for you and your children.

Genesis 50:20–21a

People ask why I do not have children. "You'd be great! Look at how they respond to you!" Yeah, except for the day when I was thirteen and I called my mom while babysitting: "I can't get her to stop crying!" as I cried myself. One hour by myself on my first job, and I knew kids weren't my gig. (By the way, the child just needed a changing.) I just don't relate well to children.

However, people still try to encourage me, "Oh, it will be different when you have your own." Maybe, but I have a hard time believing it.

I've accepted the thought, with glee, that I might not be a soccer mom armed with cleats and orange slices. I have come to terms that I might not have the pleasure of watching the odometer climb as I take kids all over the planet, praying that there's not an allergic reaction to peanut butter sticky fingers in the back seat. Most importantly, I thank God each day that I did not have kids involved during my separation.

Maybe your house smells like macaroni and cheese. Maybe last year's ketchup stain is a loving reminder of how much fun *Sesame Street* and hotdogs can be during lunchtime. Just perhaps, the empty car seat in the garage is yet another reminder of the season of life God cooked up for you right now.

God loves children. Much more than I do. He relishes in the spilled relish. He yearns for the sharp cry, "Dad!" God loves to have fun and watch His children grow. I know this because when Joseph met up with his brothers, the theme of the story hibernates in families. The background of Joseph draws out how much God loves children, even to those of us who have none.

Joseph's story climaxes when Joseph makes a proclamation: "You intended to harm me, but God intended it for good to accomplish what is now being done, the saving of many lives. So then, don't be afraid, I will provide for you and your children" (Genesis 50:20-21a). Joseph met with his siblings but first made sure to eliminate any fears. What fear could ruin their strength in unity? Their families would be left behind. Their families would not be provided for if left behind. As a great example of leadership, God gave Joseph the desire to help children. God will take care of your children too. Now that is something I can relate to; God, my Father, will take care of my family and me.

Whether your family is together or physically apart, be assured in Genesis 50. Reading the chapter and arriving at the finale can prompt the separated person to be delighted that God takes care of families. He "will provide for you and your children."

Father God,

You state that things hurt, even if I'm in a place where it becomes clear that You meant it for good. Take care of my family as I work out what You have for me on this path.

20
Reach for God

The name of the Lord is a fortified tower; the righteous run to it and are safe.

Proverbs 18:10

My finger hovered over the button to change the station on the drive home from work. Then *that* song came on, releasing my finger. I looked at the road ahead and saw it start to wave through the moisture in my eyes. It was a horrific sound as I sang through the tears, but it was joyful. Singing that song became a release. I'd hum it if no one were around at work or home.

A favorite band of mine wrote a song to God about His protective qualities: how He is our strength. I needed His strength. I remember few occasions where verbal pushing accelerated into physical pushing. A year after the separation began, I still felt pushed emotionally.

Fortunately, my Savior knows me the best. He knows which song kept me going and brought me comfort. In that season, anything about being safe perked my ears. Being safe in God's care calmed my nerves that had been seared with emotional pain like a hot razor blade.

Once when I was on the phone, again in the car with the radio turned up, I spoke with a friend in a similar situation. It was important for me to talk to someone I could trust, someone hundreds of miles away. When the song came on, I told her we'd finish chatting another day, and she promptly said, "No! Turn it up, this is my song!" Our colorful singing over the phone must have looked nuts to other drivers, but I was safe. Safe with God, and safe with my friend.

God speaks through many avenues, mostly unexpected turns while driving through pain in life. Running to God and feeling safe is important when being in a house full of angst. I used worship music as an escape, a reminder of God's presence in a silent season.

Find a way to reach out to Him, something to run to when it gets scary.

<u>Lord</u>,

I'm going to run to You. Please be my protection. Thank you for offering that to me.

21
Find Yourself in God

For your Maker is your husband—the Lord Almighty is his name—the Holy One of Israel is your Redeemer; he is called the God of all the earth.

Isaiah 54:5

Two weeks had passed since I'd left. I needed some space to find out what I was doing that caused the separation and to find out if I wanted to make it work. I also wanted to see what his default setting was because when you are away from your spouse, you will fall into the most natural of habits for you. I wanted to know what those habits were for him.

My default habits included throwing myself into work. I found what I thought would be a perfect role and perfect distraction for me right away. I stopped by a TV station since that's what I had done for a living in previous positions. The interview was a flop.

The rejection was fresh when a friend called. My teetering emotions already raw, my friend's thoughtfulness pushed me into a fresh wave of tears. "I was just in the mall with my sister, and we found a store that should have been named after you. It had all kinds of organizational items, boxes and totes, baskets and purses. I so wish you could have seen it."

My throat closed up, and I held back tears. I cried inside, not because she wanted to experience that with me but because she knew a part of myself I had forgotten. I didn't remember that I loved cute boxes, cubbyholes, and baskets. A store filled with organizational items is something I would have enjoyed—before marriage. I had forgotten who I was in my pursuit of living a "normal" married life.

I had not only forsaken who I was, but Whose I was. I didn't remember that I was a child of God and that He would take care of me with or without the pursuit of work.

Isaiah 54 is a chapter I read daily, and from which I eventually memorized key sections. It was powerful to realize that God is my Spouse. God—the One who redeemed me for eternity, Who tells the trees to sway, Who organized the stars—is my Husband.

Whether my spouse and I chose to be together again or not, my default setting should be found in God. My identity belongs to my Redeemer. The separation provided me space to not only rediscover myself and how I like to live, but also Who my God is and how He wants me to serve. I can use my talents to increase God's Kingdom. I can do what I love to express my love to my Redeemer. Maybe working isn't the greatest of defaults, but organization is something I can do to help His Kingdom.

What is your default setting? Take a moment to think of how those individual characteristics can be used as a form of worship to your Eternal Spouse.

God,

<u>Li</u>ving on my own means finding a new identity. I pray that identity is wrapped up solely in You and that I can find the best way to bring You glory. Thank You for being a source of encouragement. I praise You for being my Redeemer.

22
I Can't Want That

I will repay you for the years the locusts have eaten—the great locust and the young locust, the other locusts and the locust swarm—my great army that I sent among you.

Joel 2:25

Twin boys went for their shots. As twins, they did everything together, so when the nurse asked, "Who wants to go first?" the twins looked at each other in unison then looked at their father.

"They don't do anything alone," he responded for both of them.

The nurse left, and the boys resumed their quiet communication between themselves, checking out the walls, pointing at pictures of cartoon lions and tigers. The doctor arrived and with soothing words and distractions, she stuck the needed medication into one toddler's arm. At first, silence, but the tears glazing his eyes pounced on his cheek in one large tear, then that tear opened his lungs as well. Father came to the rescue to hold his son and give encouragement. Toddler number two looked at the doctor and said, "I can't want that."

For so long I kept seeing divorce and saying to myself, "I can't want that." It wasn't until I sat in the lawyer's office, watching a lady leave with a big tear glazing her eye as she wrote a check that I realized I wasn't toddler number two; I was the first twin to get a shot. I had no idea what I was getting into, but I wanted some control over what had eaten away at me for years—a lack of control and freedom to choose who I was.

Being separated cut my identity in half. My identity had been being married. I was a wife. But now, I was just alone. I didn't know who I was. I lost myself.

I found myself in today's verse from the book of Joel. A great army can overwhelm, but the fields will come back stronger than ever. I had lost personality traits and most importantly, the identity of being a child of God. God repaid me for the years I lost. I can want that!

Now is the time to explore you, whether the best choice is to return or to continue being apart from your spouse. In either case, be confident in Christ. Find out new ways you can serve Him that perhaps were not available before. New friends, new groups, and maybe a few old relationships can be revisited. Take hold of the choice to say, "I can want that."

Father,

I may have lost some of me, but I have gained You. Fill me so that when it is my time to get a shot or do something I can't want, I do not have to fear. Bring my identity closer to Yours and repay me for our lost time together.

23
Finding Answers

Whether you turn to the right or to the left, your ears will
hear a voice behind you, saying, "This is the way; walk in it."

Isaiah 30:21

On February 1, 2010, I did not go to work. Instead, I had a hotdog at a restaurant. I didn't feel hungry since anxiety filled my belly. The tasteless hotdog still filled me physically, and it filled the time I had to wait. Just a few more hours of waiting, after years of waiting. Then divorce would be final.

I thought months before the time the court day came that I would have figured out whether the divorce was the way to go or not. I thought I would know before I even went to the lawyer's office for the first time six months earlier. People from church asked questions like, "Are you initiating it?" I suppose they wanted to know if I was following their interpretation of Scripture. Some wanted to know his spiritual status, and others wanted to hear the reasons why—abuse or an affair? No reason? In the end, I determined it was God's answers that mattered most.

My supportive friends and I finished our lunch and got in the car. At one point while driving to the courthouse, I remember saying, "I still don't know if I am doing the right thing." And you know what the voice behind me said?

"Yes, you are doing the right thing." My friend in the car gave me that final confidence when I couldn't trust my own thoughts.

Not every situation is the same. Not every divorce is okay, and not every divorce is bad. What I do know is that in the hardest of moments, when the confidence hides, someone will tune into God to be that voice that says, "This is the way; walk in it." Seek out people who seek God and encourage you to ask God about your situation. Especially on days when the hotdogs seem tasteless and the anxiety is overwhelming.

Lord Jesus,

I want to put my trust in You. Will You speak to me about what the next step is for me? I want to hear Your voice, and I want to walk in Your ways. Be loud if You need to. Be my Guide.

24
Expect Troubles

*But those who marry will face many troubles in this life,
and I want to spare you this.*

1 Corinthians 7:28b

"So expect troubles, Mollie," is what I wrote next to this verse. While it's true that a married individual should expect troubles, my previous interpretation of this verse was that I would expect troubles, but my spouse would not—that my spouse was the source of troubles, which put me in a me-versus-him mentality. My misinterpretation backfired severely. I thought this verse excused poor behavior and controlling characteristics. I thought every marriage had years of nastiness before mellowing out to a loving relationship. As one of the few in my group of friends that married young, I figured it was just a trial to go through.

A friend of mine, Joanna, experienced similar troubles which may be why I thought all marriages were troublesome from the start. Joanna's spouse decided she had too many things. So, he threw all her shoes from the middle of a bridge over a river, tied her to a chair in her now empty closet, and pointed a gun at her head telling her about the number of possessions she could have. I would not count that as the troubles that this verse talks about. That is abuse. If you are escaping this kind of situation, be encouraged. You will be healthier spiritually, mentally, and physically this day forward.

Yet if you did not experience an abusive situation, still carefully heed these words of Scripture. I once manipulated, used tears as bullets, and held hidden agendas. Troubles in a marriage are like troubles when you are single. Either side of the fence will bring loneliness, an unfulfilled soul, bad attitudes, and improper motivations. That points to patterns within yourself and not with the situation. Whether the victim or abuser of boundaries, this verse doesn't endorse poor choices.

Joanna's counselor, while she was still married, asked if she was being abused. Joanna answered no, thinking that everyone had at least a similar experience. "Isn't that what submitting was all about?" she asked.

Fortunately, Joanna told me that her counselor didn't answer that question. Instead, the counselor's response was, "What does the Bible say about it?" Which sent Joanna on the quest to understand.

Joanna ended up moving to a new state to get some physical distance between her and her husband. Her new pastor asked her to look at people she knew who are married. What do they complain about? What do other couples argue about? What are their troubles like?

Joanna told me about the moment that it all became clear to her. She walked into work and heard a colleague get off the phone with a huff. "He left his lunch on the counter, and I can't get it to him. The meat is going to rot sitting there!"

"That's it?" she thought. "Is that really a trouble?" During one argument, Joanna's spouse posed sanctions on grocery money. She ate beans and rice, and he secretly went to a fast-food restaurant with a buddy.

Joanna explained another "ah-ha" moment. A co-worker had to get her children to gymnastics practice, and her husband wasn't answering the phone. Mostly because he was still asleep. She was furious and told him this was important to their children. He apologized and made it up to her by having dinner ready when she got home. At Joanna's home, sleeping until 4 or 5 in the afternoon was okay for her spouse as long as *she* had a meal ready after her work hours. Joanna, like myself, thought our situations were the trouble Paul was talking about in this verse. Yet, the poor behaviors exhibited had nothing to do with this verse.

The verse was all about me. Did I turn to Jesus when troubles arose? Was I trying to find satisfaction and contentment in marriage? Troubles over general life difficulties, emotional needs, and other issues were my own, to be sorted out by me and God, not me and my husband. If you look to Jesus with your spouse, you'll see that there is reason to, "Take heart, [He] has overcome the world" (John 16:33b). Whether you are single or married, expect troubles in this life.

"Time is short," Paul says in 1 Corinthians 7:29. Take his word on it. During the time you are away, it is a chance for you to evaluate the motivations, attitudes, and actions of your troubles. Are they troubles resulting from marriage or troubles from being human?

God,

You didn't promise an easy life. I see that now that I am away. Show me the parts that need to change so I don't repeat these troubles in my future, whether single or married. Help me to take note of healthy relationships I see around me. I'm so glad You are with me, even now.

25
Opinions

The one who eats everything must not treat with contempt the one who does not, and the one who does not eat everything must not judge the one who does, for God has accepted them. Who are you to judge someone else's servant? To their own master, servants stand or fall. And they will stand, for the Lord is able to make them stand.

Romans 14:3-4

My friend asked me if it was appropriate for her to take communion. She reasoned that God hated divorce, and she was recently—unwillingly—divorced. It's a difficult question, a question to bring to the Lord.

Her question brought to mind the verse from Romans. It's not my place to judge your situation. It is my place to encourage you to stand for what you know is right and true according to Scripture. Whether divorce or reconciliation is right for you and your spouse is nothing that friends, family, or other believers can guide you in the truth by offering their opinions.

Everyone has opinions. It's like when you get in a car accident and you share it with a friend. That friend feels compelled to sympathize with you by sharing a story about someone else's or their own car wreck. During separation, your friends may be well-intentioned, but perhaps misguided, in thinking that hearing about other's separation will be a balm to your soul. At least that's how it was for me.

No matter what your situation is—the length, the process, or even the circumstances—those around you may want to help make you feel better. Hearing of others' situations may help and it may hurt. If it is sensitive, it is okay to politely shift the conversation away from your own pain: "Thanks for sharing your story. This is sensitive for me, and I think it's best for me to chat about something else." You can also be open to hearing their tale because a new revelation may come through the story. Still, it's acceptable to be honest about how you feel. Romans teaches that each man is accepted by God. Since God is man's Master, then I cannot be his master. Whether a man or a woman is a believer, I am not in control of their decisions, even if they hurt me. God's opinion is the one that matters.

God,

It is hard to avoid the things that hurt me. It's hard to not want to judge anyone's situation as truth. But You are my Master, and I want nothing more than to please You, so please be with me as those thoughts arise.

26
Finding Your Inner Circle

The wise prevail through great power, and those who have knowledge muster their strength. Surely you need guidance to wage war, and victory is won through many advisers.

Proverbs 24:5–6

As I looked around the table, I thought, "Really? Is this the last session?" Each person I saw sitting at that table had heard my story. Each person had shown a side to healing I hadn't understood without their words of wisdom. Since this was the last gathering of our small band of divorcees, I felt the sting of loneliness again. I'd have to walk on my own now but with the strength and wisdom I found around the table. Loneliness stood right outside the door, but I had one final weapon because of the healing I experienced in the company of others.

After moving to a new city, I was able to test out in public what I learned while being separated. In the new town, I found a church that provided eight-week sessions for those experiencing divorce. Although at this time I had been divorced for a few years, I thought I'd be a good source of encouragement for others. I thought my healing was complete, and I would not learn anything new.

Instead, I found myself soaking up more knowledge and becoming a stronger single as the weeks progressed. The key lesson for me was that healing takes many forms. Some learned best by listening. Others healed by talking through their own experience. We all learned and healed by opening ourselves to God. I learned to wage war against loneliness by having those new friends gather around me week by week.

Although much is learned by being intimate with the Creator of life, life is also found in groups. Who is a part of your community? Grab a pen. Draw three circles below, one inside the other with enough room to write in the blank spaces. Who is in your most inner circle? Who do you call when it's super late at night? Who knows what you are feeling? Who are you smiling about right now? Enter those names in the smallest innermost circle. The next circle out should include those who know about your situation. Who do you consider valuable in your life but not essential to recovery? Finally, the last circle is those who are not part of your inner circles. Who is not invited to know all your secrets? Who might not be the person you would trust revealing all bits of your situation because they are not part of the most trusted people in your life?

Find some trusted advisers and keep them in the center of your circle.

God,

I want victory, whether it be over loneliness or another emotion or situation I am dealing with. Be the core of my center and use Your power in my life.

27
God's Restoration

And the God of all grace, who called you to his eternal glory in Christ, after you have suffered a little while, will himself restore you and make you strong, firm and steadfast.

1 Peter 5:10

I sat on the bed, staring at the closet, mentally taking each item, trying it on, putting it back. I was also mentally practicing answers to the questions I'd be answering at the interview. I'd been divorced for almost two years, and I still had a hard time seeing myself being able to earn more than barely paying the bills. I had applied for a job that could become a new career, far from the paycheck-to-paycheck lifestyle and back in an industry I loved. However, the phone interview put a new spin on the answers I would give at the in-person interview.

The station called about a week ago. The first questions, about past employment, were easy to answer. However, this application actually asked if I was divorced, and being an honest person, I checked yes, reading the disclosure that questions pertaining to the divorce could arise during the interview. When the station called for a preliminary interview, the questions about my divorce didn't rise like nice flowers; they felt like low ground cover, out to kill off the fresh growth in my life. I tried, honestly but discreetly, to answer the questions. They wanted to know the "issues" that caused the "geographical separation." How much is appropriate to talk about without them hearing both sides of the story? More to the point, how much of my divorce is going to affect my work ability? Why not question all my past sins or past relationships?

I had a friend who worked at a coffee shop located at a church years ago. When they heard she had thought about starting divorce proceedings, they fired her. I didn't think I would be in a situation like that, where your marital status held the key to earning a living.

Peter says after a "little while" of suffering, God restores. God doesn't hold every choice against us. He's not about works alone. He's about grace.

Whether I got the job or found the perfect outfit, the important note I mentally took with me in my pocket to the interview is that God makes me "strong, firm and steadfast."

The marital status checkbox on the medical form, the application, or the tax form is just a box created by humans. God wipes out boxes so that He can restore us to full strength. Even during an interview. (An interview that led to full-time employment.)

Father,

Some things in my future make it seem as though the suffering will last forever. I am grateful that You are the Restorer and that You work beyond our boxes. Help me to see how You are making me stronger, even today.

28
Benediction

May the Lord answer you when you are in distress; may the name of the God of Jacob protect you. May he send you help from the sanctuary and grant you support from Zion . . . Now this I know: the Lord gives victory to his anointed. He answers him from his heavenly sanctuary with the victorious power of his right hand. Some trust in chariots and some in horses, but we trust in the name of the Lord our God.

Psalm 20:1–2, 6–7

As we part ways, there are a few last moments to spend in precious prayer. My prayer echoes Psalm 20, especially the verses for today. When your heart bleeds, I pray He finds and heals the crack. I pray your church supports you or that you find a good group of people to support you. I pray God saves you and that He shows you that He's got you, that there's nothing to fear. We trust in God, and that's good enough.

The blank space below is for you. Take a moment, write a prayer, journal about the lesson you want to remember about the most, spout some emotions—it's your page to express what you have learned, felt, or healed from this past month. Even if all you have time—or energy—for is one sentence, feel free to do so; it's your page. Maybe copy down the verses above. Sometimes seeing a verse in your handwriting makes it personal and memorable.

Friend, thank you for the journey and keep pursuing God.

Acknowledgments

Someone wrote that "Authors write by themselves, but they never are truly alone in the journey and process." Many people have traveled with me on the journey that produced what you hold in your hands. I'm thanking as many as I can here, but if I were to thank everyone, it would be a book about gratitude rather than hope during a separation! Next time.

First, thanks be to God, the true Author. Keeping our eyes on Him is the first (and only) next step toward perfecting faith (Hebrews 12:2). If the encouragement and hope you feel are greater because you have gotten closer to Christ in this journey, then I have done my job and remained obedient.

Thanks to my husband, James, who was the first to call me an author and one of the first avid readers of my blogs. Your continued support and encouragement get me moving toward our dreams (and up at 4:44 am to write).

I am deeply grateful for the bravery of the people who allowed me to share their stories. You know who you are!

This journey truly began ten years ago. To my friends at Harvest Bible Chapel in Davenport, including Paula and Dave Olsen, and Jonny: thank you for your support. Thanks to all my Kansas friends, especially Big and Little Crystal, Joyce, Shirley, Melinda, and Deb. Thanks to the Hope for Haiti board who allowed me to use my writing to support the good work in the St. Marc region of Haiti.

Thank you to friends I met through my grant proposal writing at Moody Bible Institute, Nonprofits on a Mission, and the Grant Professionals

Association. It is my grant proposal writing skills that brought my "hobby" writing to a new level. Thank you for taking a risk on me and mentoring me along the way: Jim Elliott, Jen Epperson, Chris Wheeler, Alene Alexander, Isik Abla, Sue Jetter, Jamie Janosz, Kelli Worrall, and Janis Todd.

And thank you to those of 4word, particularly Pat Asp, Kathryn Tack, and Diane Paddison. Diane, it is your book, *Work, Love, Pray,* that helped me see I wasn't alone in the journey and that women who have been separated can still have worthwhile careers. Thank you for that example.

Thank you to Welby O'Brien, whose book truly changed my perspective from "It's not possible to survive" to "I think I might just thrive."

Thanks to my writing buddies, who graciously gave of their time and skill to help me hone my craft. Especially to those of what I've dubbed in my mind the "Yellow Box Church Crew:" Kristina Cowan, Christy Brunke, and Anthony "Tony" Trendl of American Speechwriters. Y'all are how I saw that this dream could be a reality.

I'm grateful to the many in the Pacific Northwest who were like, "Mollie, seriously, get that book printed!" Thank you, Kari Trent Stageberg, Beth A. Lewis, Elliot Stockstad, Kate Gerkin, Sarah Kardelen, and Dwight Vick.

To my friends of the 21-day challenge of 2020: Becky DeVries, Cathy Sywulka, Paige Shope, and Jen Ilchishin. Thank you for that month that built the habit I maintain today.

Thank you to my parents, who were the first to call and share the excitement about this book. Many more calls like that to come.

And thank you, dear reader, for allowing me to be part of your journey. If you have received any encouragement, please let me know! You'll find me @Hopeful_Bond on Twitter and @HopelesslyHopefulBooks on Facebook. Read more blogs and bonus devotionals at molliebond.org.

Bibliography

O'Brien, Welby. *Formerly a Wife: A Survival Guide for Women Facing the Pain and Disruption of Divorce.* Camp Sherman, OR: Trusted Books, 1996.

For more information about

Mollie Bond
and
Hopelessly Hopeful During Separation
please visit:

www.HopelesslyHopefulBooks.com

Ambassador International's mission is to magnify the Lord Jesus Christ and promote His gospel through the written word.

We believe through the publication of Christian literature, Jesus Christ and His Word will be exalted, believers will be strengthened in their walk with Him, and the lost will be directed to Jesus Christ as the only way of salvation.

For more information about
AMBASSADOR INTERNATIONAL
please visit:

www.ambassador-international.com

Thank you for reading this book. Please consider leaving us a review on your social media, favorite retailer's website, Goodreads or Bookbub, or our website.

More from Ambassador International...

Destination Hope is a must-read invaluable guide, offering hope and sound wisdom for your unpredictable, individual life journeys. Written by two of the wisest tried, tested, and true women of God—April White and Marilyn Nutter—you will see how each author poured out beautiful transparency. Like two best friends who've trailed the hard ground before you, April and Marilyn, seem to gently take you by the hand and lead you toward God's heart for healing.

We interact with people every day whether it be with our coworkers, family, friends—life is filled with relationships! While not all relationships are good, with God's help, we can work to better our current and future relationships and overcome the effects of toxic relationships.

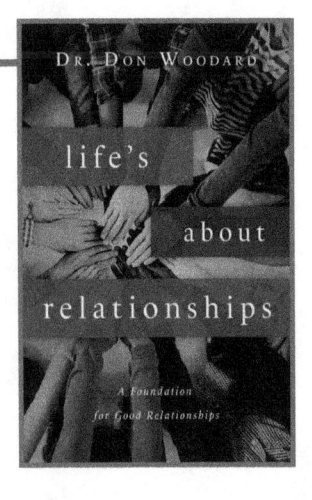

As we walk through dark times in our lives, we all need a way of *Finding Truth in the Tempest.* Faythelma Bechtel knows the tempest, but she also knows the One Who calms the storm. After losing two daughters and her husband, Faythelma has clung tighter to her Savior and longs to help others who are struggling to find peace in their own storms. This devotional journal is not meant to be read as a daily plan, but instead offers meditations on Scripture to help for your unique circumstance.